Whales/Ballenas

By Valerie J. Weber

Reading Consultant: Susan Nations, M.Ed.,
author/literacy coach/consultant in literacy development/

Consultora de lectura: Susan Nations, M.Ed.,
autora/tutora de alfabetización/consultora de desarrollo de lectoescritura

WEEKLY READER®
PUBLISHING

Please visit our web site at www.garethstevens.com.
For a free catalog describing our list of high-quality books,
call 1-800-542-2595 (USA) or 1-800-387-3178 (Canada).
Our fax: 1-877-542-2596

Library of Congress Cataloging-in-Publication Data

Weber, Valerie.
    (Whales. Spanish & English)
    Whales = Ballenas / by/por Valerie J. Weber ; reading consultant/
consultora de lectura, Susan Nations.
        p. cm. — (Animals that live in the ocean = Animales que viven en el océano)
    Includes bibliographical references and index.
    ISBN-10: 0-8368-9569-X   ISBN-13: 978-0-8368-9569-8 (lib. bdg.)
    ISBN-10: 0-8368-9579-7   ISBN-13: 978-0-8368-9579-7 (softcover)
    1. Whales—Juvenile literature. I. Title. II. Title: Ballenas.
QL737.C4W38818   2009
599.5—dc22   2008017704

This edition first published in 2009 by
Weekly Reader® Books
An Imprint of Gareth Stevens Publishing
1 Reader's Digest Road
Pleasantville, NY 10570-7000 USA

Copyright © 2009 by Gareth Stevens, Inc.

Senior Managing Editor: Lisa M. Herrington
Senior Editor: Barbara Bakowski
Creative Director: Lisa Donovan
Designer: Alexandria Davis
Cover Designer: Amelia Favazza, *Studio Montage*
Photo Researcher: Diane Laska-Swanke
Translation: Tatiana Acosta and Guillermo Gutiérrez

Photo Credits: Cover, pp. 7, 9, 11, 15, 17, 19 © SeaPics.com;
p. 1 © Chua Han Hsiung/Shutterstock; p. 5 © Digital Vision;
p. 13 © Doug Perrine/naturepl.com; p. 21 © Sue Flood/naturepl.com

Printed in the United States of America

1 2 3 4 5 6 7 8 9 10 09 08

Table of Contents

- - - - - - - - - - - -

Contenido

Boldface words appear in the glossary./
Las palabras en **negrita** aparecen en el glosario.

Who Is This Giant?

A huge tail lifts out of the sea. Down comes the tail, slapping the water. What kind of animal has a tail so big?

- - - - - - - - - - - - - - -

¿Quién es este gigante?

Una enorme cola se levanta sobre el mar. Ahora cae, golpeando el agua. ¿Qué animal tiene una cola tan grande?

4

Whales can be very big! The blue whale is the world's largest animal. It is as long as three school buses in a row!

- - - - - - - - - - - - - - - -

¡Las ballenas pueden ser muy grandes! La ballena azul es el animal más grande del mundo. ¡Mide lo mismo que tres autobuses escolares puestos en fila!

blue whale/
ballena azul

7

A Breath of Fresh Air

Many other kinds of whales swim in the ocean. Like people, they need to breathe air. They come to the top of the water to breathe.

- - - - - - - - - - - - - -

Un poco de aire puro

Muchos otros tipos de ballenas nadan en el océano. Igual que las personas, las ballenas necesitan aire. Para respirar, suben a la superficie del agua.

A whale breathes through its **blowhole**. The animal squirts water and air out of the blowhole. Its spray flies high in the air.

- - - - - - - - - - - - -

Una ballena respira por su **espiráculo**. Por ahí lanza agua y aire. Ese chorro sube muy alto.

Baby Whales and Adult Whales

A baby whale is called a **calf**. It is born underwater. The mother whale pushes the calf to the surface for its first breath.

- - - - - - - - - - - - - -

Ballenas adultas, crías de ballena

La cría de ballena recibe el nombre de **ballenato**. Nace bajo el agua. La madre empuja al ballenato hacia la superficie para que tome aire por primera vez.

calf/
ballenato

A mother whale feeds its calf milk. A whale calf drinks 50 gallons of milk each day. Could you drink that much milk?

- - - - - - - - - - - - - -

El ballenato se alimenta de la leche de la madre. Un ballenato bebe 50 galones de leche al día. ¿Podrían ustedes beber tanta leche?

Some adult whales eat tiny plants and animals called **plankton** (PLANK-tuhn). A whale gulps huge amounts of water and plankton. The whale lets out the water through its mouth.

- - - - - - - - - - - - - -

Algunas ballenas adultas comen **plancton**, formado por diminutas plantas y animales. Una ballena se traga grandes cantidades de agua y plancton. Después, suelta el agua por la boca.

mouth/
boca

Other whales chase big groups of fish. A whale opens its mouth wide around the fish. Then the whale snaps its mouth shut.

- - - - - - - - - - - - - - -

Otras ballenas persiguen a grupos grandes de peces. La ballena abre la boca sobre los peces. Después, la cierra de golpe.

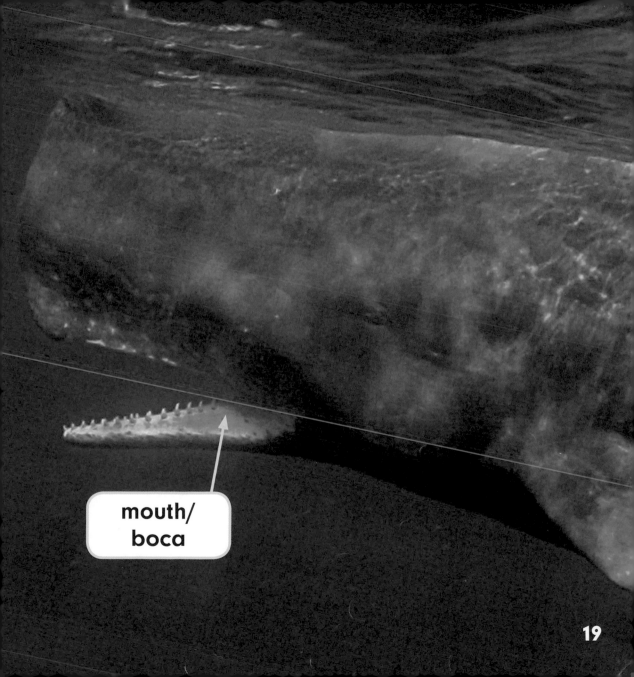

mouth/
boca

19

Long Trips

Many kinds of whales travel far every year. They swim from warm seas to cold seas. There, they find plenty of fish and plankton to eat.

- - - - - - - - - - - - - - -

Largos viajes

Muchos tipos de ballenas recorren grandes distancias cada año. Nadan de mares cálidos a mares fríos. Allí encuentran mucho pescado y plancton para comer.

Glossary/Glosario

blowhole: opening on top of a whale's head through which it breathes air

calf: a baby whale or other animal

plankton: small animals and plants that live in water

- - - - - - - - - - - - - -

ballenato: ballena joven

espiráculo: abertura en la parte superior de la cabeza de una ballena, que el animal usa para respirar

plancton: pequeños animales y plantas que viven en el agua

For More Information/Más información

Books/Libros

The Blue Whale: The World's Largest Animal/La ballena azul: El mamífero más grande. Joy Paige (Rosen Publishing Group, 2003)

Whales/Ballenas. My World of Animals/Mi mundo de animales (series). Frances E. Ruffin (PowerKids Press, 2004)

Web Sites/Páginas web

Whales at Enchanted Learning/Ballenas en Enchanted Learning
www.enchantedlearning.com/subjects/whales
Learn all kinds of facts about whales, and print whale outlines to color!/Aprendan todo tipo de datos sobre las ballenas, ¡e impriman siluetas de ballenas para colorear!

Whale Times: Fishin' for Facts/Whale Times: Pescando información
www.whaletimes.org/whales.htm
Learn about the different parts of a whale./Conozcan las diferentes partes de una ballena.

Index/Índice

About the Author

A writer and editor for 25 years, Valerie Weber especially loves working in children's publishing. The variety of topics is endless, from weird animals to making movies. It is her privilege to try to engage children in their world through books.

Información sobre la autora

A Valerie Weber, que ha sido escritora y editora durante 25 años, le gusta sobre todo trabajar en libros infantiles. La variedad de temas es inagotable: desde insólitos animales hasta cómo se hace una película. Para ella es un privilegio tratar de interesar a los niños en el mundo por medio de sus libros.